Myself When Young

Myself When Young

by

Florence M. Ratcliffe

The Pentland Press Ltd.
Edinburgh · Cambridge · Durham

First Published in 1991 by
The Pentland Press Ltd.
Brockerscliffe
Witton le Wear
Durham

ISBN 1 872795 42 0

Typeset by Spire Origination, Norwich.
Printed and bound by Antony Rowe Ltd., Chippenham.
Jacket design by Geoff Hobbs

Contents

Chapter 1

Random Recollections

There is nothing more scaring than the unknown; the unseen and mysterious presence at which one cannot strike back. Though never a nervous person, I recall one incident in my early childhood when I nearly 'passed out' with fright.

Always an inveterate reader, one night I was so engrossed in a book that I sneaked it upstairs with me when I went to bed. At the time, I was sleeping in one of the attic bedrooms, which I usually shared with my little sister Mary, then about five years old. Sometimes, however, she slept with another sister in one of the other bedrooms, and on entering my room on this particular night I saw that the bed was empty. I got undressed and, since it was impossible to read in bed, I sat on a chair near the fireplace in order to continue my book by the only light available. It came from a small gas jet with a burner something like a bullet, which gave out a little fan-shaped flame. As my parents slept in the room underneath, I had to be as quiet and still as possible. Otherwise they would have known that I was not in bed and getting my beauty sleep and would have called out to me to put out the light.

Absorbed in my book, I sat getting colder and colder and probably straining my eyes, when suddenly I heard the stairs creaking. My first thought was that my father had at last determined to teach me a lesson. I stood up in anticipation but no footsteps could I hear; just a creaking on each step of the stairs. I believe it was twelve steps that I counted as I waited for the door to open, but it did not. Instead came four slow knocks, then...nothing! I have said that I had become cold while reading, but now I absolutely froze. Waves like melting ice rippled over me from head to foot. The eeriness of those strange knocks had paralyzed me. It took only a few seconds, I suppose, for me to think of something to do, but it seemed like an eternity. Then some subconscious instinct prompted me quietly to slip the catch on the door, thereby giving myself time to think and recover my failing senses. What I

feared I had no idea. I knew it couldn't be Father. He would have come straight in
— no knocking or waiting outside for him!

"Well," I thought, "I can't stand here all night. I must be brave and open the
door — I can always shout!" In fact I doubt whether I could have made a sound.
However, with this thought I summoned up all my courage and swung the door
back. In walked a small figure in white; it calmly swept passed me and climbed into
bed. My amazement was equalled only by my relief. It was Mary; she had been
walking in her sleep! To my knowledge, she was the only member of the family
ever to do so. After all, one somnambulist is enough for any family!

One of Mary's companions was the schoolmaster's son, a boy of about her own
age who used to live a few doors away from us. One day, a year or two before the
sleep-walking episode, they were playing together on a piece of waste land outside
the house of Mrs Bury, our next-door neighbour. Hearing the children scream, Mrs
Bury looked out of her window to see Mary's dress on fire. Fortunately she had
been meaning to swill down her steps and had just drawn a bucket of water for that
purpose. She rushed out and threw the water over Mary, probably saving her life
thereby. Then came the explanations. They had gone into our outside wash-house,
it seems, and had climbed up so as to reach a high shelf where Mother kept a box of
matches. One would have felt sure that in such a place they were out of reach of
little fingers, but in this case the children's determination had defeated all precau-
tions. If such a disaster had happened today, Mary would have been sent to hospital,
but in those days things were different. Though very ill for some time and surely
suffering considerable pain, she was simply kept at home. She always bore the
scars of this misadventure, and I think that her very infrequent bouts of sleep-
walking were probably due to the upset to her nerves occasioned by it.

This reminds me of another terrible misadventure with a child. It happened not to
us but to a certain Mrs Townley who used to come and do the washing etc. She had
several children and as her husband was out of work they were very poor. They had
come to Oswaldtwistle from Morecambe, where he had been employed as a plas-
terer. To earn a little extra money he had been doing one or two jobs in the evening,
but when his Union discovered this they took away his Union card. That meant that
he found it almost impossible to obtain any work at all.

The Townleys were very decent people but so poor that Mrs T. used to ask
Mother for our empty jam jars, which in those days were made out of a sort of rough
pottery. They used these instead of cups and would have been in fashion today, now
that thick crockery has become so popular. Sometimes Mrs Townley would bring
her youngest child, a little boy, with her and one day on entering the drawing-room
the coal-scuttle caught his eye. Never having seen one before, with childish

curiosity he opened the lid to reveal the coal inside. "Eh," he exclaimed in surprise, "What a little coyle-nook!"

On one occasion Mrs T. found Mother baking. She had kneaded the dough and had left it in front of the kitchen fire to rise. Mrs T. was horrified. "Oh!" she cried, "don't leave your bowl on the floor — always put it on a stool or something!" It seems that as a result of leaving her dough to rise by the fire she had had the terrible experience of losing a child. Leaving her two year-old son in the room on the floor (the usual place for dough to be put to rise), she had run across the road to get some currants from a shop. She returned to find that the child had fallen head first into the dough and been smothered. Ever since, she said, she couldn't bear to see a bowl of dough on the floor. Poor woman, it was hardly surprising — how she must have suffered!

Mother had a friend called Lisbeth Ann. They had known each other since early girlhood days, when they had gone to school together. When L.A. married she went to live in Blackburn, so that her visits to our house were somewhat infrequent. She had two children, a girl and a boy. The girl was a thoroughly nice child, but the boy was a veritable imp. One had to keep a watchful eye on Bobby whenever he came with his mother; to fail to do so would prove highly unwise. One day L.A. and my mother were in the drawing-room enjoying a cup of tea (spiced, no doubt, with a certain amount of gossip) when suddenly L.A. remarked: "Heavens, I'd forgotten our Bobby! Goodness knows what he'll be up to — I told him to play outside for a while!" Out she went and soon found him. He was no further away than the back garden, but he had been BUSY! Our house had two front doors each equipped with its own large brass knob together with a letterbox and yale lock, also in brass. On the gate was a brass plate informing any interested party that the name of our house was 'Fair View'. Somewhere Bobby had found a brush and had painted all these brass fittings with mud and clay. "Oh Bobby!" exclaimed his mother. Since it often fell to me to clean the brass, I could have reminded her of a lot more appropriate words! However, being a well brought up girl, I did not utter them until the visitors had departed.

Fortunately my brother Willie was a quite different character. Soon after we had gone to live in Stanhill Lane he had joined the Boy Scouts. The troop to which he belonged was the first to be formed in Oswaldtwistle and to most of the people there scouting was quite a novel idea. The founder of the movement, Baden Powell, would, I'm sure, have been highly gratified had he known what enthusiasm his scheme had engendered in our house. Willie, the only member of the family eligible to join, was quite keen; he loyally attended all the required meetings, carried out all the duties etc. However, if his interest may be likened to a spark, mine was, by comparison, like an Olympic torch. I was obsessed! I loved this scouting business, but of course all my keenness was wasted; females were unwanted, unnoticed and unloved. My parents gave Willie every encouragement and we began to take the appropriate weekly paper, 'The Scout'. It used to arrive on Thursdays and Father had first 'go' at it, reading it through while we impatiently waited our turns. As the only scout in the house, Willie had the paper after Father, while I came third. How we all looked forward to the next episode in the current serial! I expect that it was only when we were all out of the house that my mother had her turn.

That was the only period in my life when I have yearned for a sex change (unheard of then)! How I longed to be a scout! My enthusiasm was equalled only by my frustration. I used lovingly to iron the brim of Willie's scout hat with sugar and water in order to stiffen it; if the weather was at all damp it soon went limp. When he started to learn semaphore I practised the signals incessantly and my mind was set on being able to signal 'S.O.S' and 'HELP'. When or how I believed that this accomplishment might be useful to me I have no idea, but I was utterly determined to master it. Willie and I used to stand on either end of the garden wall and practise signalling to each other. To any passer-by we must have looked highly peculiar as we waved our arms about like maniacs. In the end Willie became fed up and refused to cooperate any further by 'reading me'.

When he became a bugler I believe that the family response was slightly less keen. In any household the noise a young boy makes in the early stages of learning to play the bugle is not conducive to euphoria! Many were the times when he was implored to "go outside to practise". Up on the moors would have been none too far away! However, that bugle signalled my downfall. Not a sound could I coax out of the obstinate thing! It was one of Willie's few triumphs over a 'big sister'. I cannot say that he achieved any great degree of proficiency, but eventually he did manage to sound 'Come to the cookhouse door' with only a few small variations upon the original tune. However, I seem to remember that the bugle was passed on to some other ignorant enthusiast before we were all driven mad. Only then was comparative peace restored to our house — and 'comparative' is the operative word!

Chapter 2

Poor Children

I am told that when I was about three years old I was lost. At so tender an age it is unlikely that I was overcome by any urge to explore the world. Probably all that happened was that I found the garden gate open and ventured out into the street, revelling in my new-found freedom. Like Felix, I must have kept on walking until eventually I was noticed by a strange lady who took me to a nearby shop. The shop belonged to a certain Moses Haworth who was my mother's uncle. He was very well known in the town, a fact which would have led my discoverer to believe that there at least I would be recognised. So there I was, perched on the counter among the other, and more saleable goods.

I can remember a woman holding me there next to a roll of cloth with a pattern of red, yellow and some other colour. As I found out later, it was Scotch plaid, but of course at the time I did not know what it was called. At all events, I took an immediate and decided dislike to that cloth, and I didn't like the woman either. As I grew older I was to learn her name. She was Uncle Moses' wife and so my aunt by marriage, though I don't remember her ever being called Aunt Alice by anyone; she was always known to us as 'Uncle Moses' wife'. I must have been recognised, for eventually my father came to claim me and take me home. To this day I still dislike that particular tartan and I never did come to like 'Uncle Moses' wife' either.

One day, some years after this incident, my mother told me: "You're going to have a new frock. Mrs Cook is going to make it for you so you'll have to go to her house to have it fitted." Of course, I was delighted. "What colour is it?" I enquired. "Scotch plaid," replied my mother, whereupon I let out a yell. "I don't like Scotch plaid," I shouted, "I won't have it, I won't wear it!"

"What do you mean, you don't like Scotch plaid?" retorted my mother, astonished at this unusual outburst, "You've never seen any! It's very nice; you'll like it when you see it. Anyway," she continued, "you're very lucky to be getting a new dress. I've bought it, so you'll have to wear it."

I cried for a while but it made no difference and eventually off I had to go to the dressmaker's. When I arrived there Mrs Cook brought out the half-made dress and — lo and behold! — it was BEAUTIFUL! Tartan, yes, but a tartan of dark green and blue. I loved it on sight and just as intensely as I had hated the one of red and yellow. That was the first time I realised that there were different patterns of tartan or, as we called it, Scotch plaid.

All this reminds me of another incident in which Uncle Moses' wife was very much concerned. It must have been holiday time, for my brother and I were not at school. We were at a loose end, strolling aimlessly along, when we finally came to a halt in front of a small corner shop not far from where we lived. The window, which was very small, was filled with all kinds of sweets. For a long time we stood there, gazing longingly at liquorice sticks, aniseed balls, lucky bags etc. — all the sweets we liked so much but which were now so unobtainable. For of course we had no money; we used to be given a penny every Saturday morning but that only lasted long enough to take it to the nearest toffee shop and exchange it for sweets. So we continued to gaze at all the delightful things in the window and the longer we looked the more we craved for them.

The road was completely empty; not a soul was in sight. Then in the distance appeared a woman advancing on the opposite side. At that point a flash of IN-SPIRATION struck me. "Go across the road," I said to my brother, "and when that lady comes up to you, you must say: 'Please can you spare a halfpenny for two poor children?'" Notice how modest I was in my demands! At first my brother de-murred, but my 'older personality' (known in the family as 'bossiness'!) prevailed, and, albeit reluctantly, he started across the road. I watched the woman stop as my brother spoke to her, and then saw her bend down to take a closer look at him. Then.... "Aren't you Willie Ashworth?" she asked. There was no denying it. She looked across the road at me, and I could tell at once by the look on her face that I had been identified as the instigator of the plot. "Well," she continued, "of all the disgraceful things — children like you begging in the street! I was just on my way to your house and we'll see what your mother has to say about this."

Off she went, and my brother came back to me on the other side of the street — needless to say, without the halfpenny. There was no need to explain to me that our scheme had failed; I had heard every word, and now we were two very frightened children. THAT WOMAN was going to tell our parents. We dared not go home, but of course in the end we had to — where else was there to go? Eventually, after many

6

hesitations, we began to trudge slowly and reluctantly back, knowing that we would have to face the music.

At that time our Auntie Maud was on a visit to the house (my mother, I imagine, would have been in the throes of one of her many pregnancies), and as Auntie opened the door to us it was plain from the expression on her face that the visitor had indeed done her worst; all had been told. Straightway we both started to cry and to beg Auntie Maud not to tell my father, but, kind as she was, this time it was all in vain. This time we had gone beyond all limits. (Fancy! Ashworth children begging in the street! Whatever would people think?)

When Father came home and was told the dire news, he at once proceeded to mete out the usual punishments. To all our noisy crying and copious tears he turned a deaf ear. Putting me over his knee in the time-honoured way, he gave my bottom a good spanking, though in fact it was not so much the pain as the sheer indignity that I felt. As for Willie, he came off better than I, for wasn't I older than he? It was I who ought to have known better; he would never have thought of doing such a thing by himself. I must have egged him on, etc. etc. All of which was probably true. Sometimes — nay, very often — being the eldest of the family was nothing but a nuisance. Always the blame, never any praise for ingenuity.

So my first attempt at extortion and 'getting rich quick' ended in miserable failure. Perhaps in fact this was a good thing. Had it been successful, I might have been tempted to take it up later as a way of life! Yet I have always felt that it was a piece of the most dismal bad luck that our very first 'victim' should have turned out to be Uncle Moses' wife. No wonder I never liked her! That it should have been precisely she of all people coming down the street at that exact moment — that surely was a fiendishly unlucky chance. However, at my present advanced age I have come to recognise that life is full of strange coincidences and hazards; there is no explaining them all.

Chapter 3

First Schooldays

I was about four years old when I first went to Trinity School. There were three infant classes: Baby Class, Second Class and First Class. After passing through all these, the children went on into a separate building known as 'The Big Room' and including Standard One to Standard Seven. The teacher of the Baby Class lived next door but one to us, so on the first morning she took me to school herself. "Well, how did you like school?" asked my mother when I returned home at midday. I replied that it had been very nice except that the teacher had called me 'Florrie', a name which I had never heard before. "You must tell Miss Bleazard that your name is not Florrie but Florence May," replied my mother with a laugh, though I don't suppose she actually expected me to be so bold as to say any such thing. Nevertheless, that afternoon, when the teacher asked me a question and addressed me as Florrie, "I'm not called Florrie — I'm called Florence May," I piped up without further ado. Several times in the course of the afternoon the same thing occurred, and I thought the teacher very forgetful, having to be told so often. Afterwards, as she talked it over with my mother, the teacher explained that she had been so amused at my indignation and persistence that she had deliberately kept on calling me Florrie just to see whether I would keep on answering her in the same way. Strangely enough, all through my schooldays every teacher called me Florrie.

Before long I was moved up from the Baby Class to the Second Class, and that was the stage at which I started to learn to write the letters of the alphabet. I loved this lesson, but for some unknown reason found myself unable to write the letter 'E'. I used to get the girl sitting next to me to make my 'E's for me.

After a few days the headmistress, Mrs Corbridge, gave me a note to take to my mother. Of course I had no knowledge of what it was about, but after reading it my mother told me its contents. Apparently the teacher said that I sometimes wet the form I sat on and asked my mother please to tell me what I must do when I wanted to go to the 'closet'. Oh yes! In those days such necessary places were known to us as 'closets'. Such refinements as 'lavatories' or 'toilets' still lay in the future, though I know that Grandma always spoke of the "doubleoo". Later I learned that this stood for 'W.C.', 'water closet'. At this point, therefore, my mother explained that when I wanted to go I must put up my hand and say: "Please may I leave the room?" (What a lot there was for a little girl to learn!).

Accordingly, the very next day I did as my mother had instructed me. "Yes," said the teacher, probably feeling that the note to my mother had not been in vain, "off you go". Leaving the class, I made my way to the cloakroom, where I stood looking round for a few moments. All I could see, however, was rows of coats and hats — not a 'closet' in sight. By this time my need was becoming urgent, so I returned to the schoolroom. "I can't find it," I said to Mrs C. At first she stared at me in disbelief. Then, "Maggie, go and show Florrie where the closets are," she said to the girl who sat next to me. Maggie took me out again, this time right through the cloakroom and into a passage leading off the yard beyond, where I could see several small doors such as might have been found on large dog-kennels. As you opened a door you found yourself facing a rough wooden seat with a hole in its centre under which was a tub. Young as I was, I was horrified, and I believe that the sight and smell of such places cured my 'weakness' and taught me sub-consciously to control my 'waterworks', for I don't remember ever again having to use those awful 'closets'. I always managed to wait until I returned home. Today at least much progress has been made in the matter of school amenities — even if not in education as such!

When I passed into the First Class I found that the girls were taught to knit. (The boys, I think, were given drawing lessons). We were equipped with thick wooden needles and brightly coloured wool. After a few weeks the teacher said: "Come out all those girls who can't knit!" Seven or eight of us left our desks and clustered round the teacher's table while she tried to show us how it was done. So far as I was concerned, it was all to no avail. Next week the number had dwindled to four non-knitters, and the week after that when she called out: "Come out anyone who still can't knit!", I alone, in deep shame, made my way to her table. She gave me a look of sheer desperation. "You can't knit yet!" she yelled, "Come over here and watch!" Taking my needles from me she began loudly to intone: "IN — OVER — THROUGH — OFF!" Several times over she repeated this refrain and suddenly it was as if the classroom was filled with a blinding light piercing its way into my non-knitting brain. Up to that moment I had been as good as the next girl at 'IN — OVER — THROUGH', but I had never yet 'OFFED'! That of course was the

9

explanation of the countless extra stitches which always appeared miraculously on my needles. Eagerly taking the wretched wool and needles, I sought to demonstrate to the teacher that I was not the cretin she had hitherto supposed. With gay abandon I 'IN — OVER — THROUGH — and OFF'ed. When she said I must stay in at playtime and practise I was delighted. No child was ever so happy to miss playtime. I COULD KNIT, and I had blissful dreams of next week using steel needles and white wool as the teacher had promised. I hope that that teacher too learned something of the art of teaching little girls to knit.

As a matter of no particular interest, in later years that same teacher became an ardent suffragette, and was one of Mrs Pankhurst's staunch followers when the suffragettes began their militant campaign, just before the First World War, in support of 'Votes for Women'.

Eventually the time came for me to be moved into 'The Big Room'. That was a great day indeed. How eagerly I had looked forward to being in Standard One! Our classroom was on an upper floor and was reached by a flight of stone stairs. Before school began, all the scholars would be playing in the school yard. Then a teacher would come to the door and blow a whistle, whereupon everybody would scuttle into lines, girls on one side, boys on the other, Standard One in front and the other classes behind. When the whistle was blown a second time Standard One would begin to march into school, the other classes following. One of the big boys was appointed Gate Monitor, and if you were not in the yard when the whistle was blown you had to wait outside the gate until all the scholars had marched into school. Only then would the Gate Monitor let you in and you would receive a 'late' mark.

Soon after being promoted to The Big Room I arrived at the gate as the scholars were marching in. Since the infants were not included in the general rule, I was not used to being kept out. I thought that the big boy was keeping me out because he thought I was an infant. This infuriated me, so I pushed past him and started to run through the yard and up the steps to our classroom, the boy panting after me. I reached the class just in front of him but by this time he was shouting: "That girl's late — she pushed in front of me! She's late!" Never before had anyone attempted to challenge his important position like this — and to be defied now by a mere chit of a girl! He must have felt like an engine driver who has just been demoted by a young ticket collector. On arriving in the classroom we caused quite a stir, but the teacher must have realised that it was all due to my new status and my resulting ignorance of 'Big Room' rules. Nothing more was said and normal peaceful conditions were soon restored. In later years the streak of independence in my character illustrated by this episode might easily have caused me to join the 'Women's Lib.' Fortunately, however, it was diverted into other channels.

There was one boy in particular whom I heartily detested, and he remained in my class from Standard One to Standard Seven. I fancy that the feeling was mutual. One day our class was out in the yard for 'drill', which in those days was the only form of 'P.T.' we underwent. We had to stand in two lines, girls in front and boys behind, and the teacher would have us bending, stretching, lungeing, marching etc. Invariably the horrible boy was just behind me. At this point I should explain that in those days little girls wore 'drawers'. These consisted of a pair of separate open legs with a band round the waist which was supported by tapes over the shoulders. I wonder now why no one thought of using elastic. We had elastic to keep our hats on and elastic garters, so why not elastic for the top of our 'drawers'? Well, back to this particular day.

All the bending, stretching etc. had proved too much for the stitches holding my tapes first on one side and then on the other. Slowly my drawers, which were made of pink flannelette of a somewhat lurid shade, began to slip down. Frantically I tried to clutch them through my dress while still attempting to go through the required routines of drill. To make matters worse, I could hear the horrid boy behind me muttering all kinds of rude things; this sort of thing gave him special delight. By this time I was in agony. My face was probably redder than the accursed drawers but what could I do? I was sure that this was the very worst thing that had ever happened to me. I felt that my drawers would soon be round my ankles. It wouldn't have been so bad if they had been my Sunday ones — white calico with lace round the bottom of the legs. Then deliverance came in the shape of Miss Yates, our teacher. "Florrie," said she, "will you please fetch my hat from the cloakroom."

As I staggered off to do her bidding, relief and gratitude flooded my entire being. I even managed somehow to tie up the fiendish tapes before finding the teacher's hat. I kept thinking how lucky I was to have been the one chosen to fetch it. Really I must have been rather dim! It was some time before I realised that the request was not prompted by any desire on the teacher's part to have a covering for her head, but was just a kindly ruse to get me out of a thoroughly awkward predicament. Nowadays little girls are at least spared from having to worry about things of that sort.

Here I must say a few words about Miss Yates. I believe she was quite a good teacher, but I'm afraid she was not very popular. In dealing out small punishments she had an unpleasant habit of poking scholars in the ribs with her 'pointer'. Schoolboys, who seem to have a marked propensity for inventing nicknames, knew her as "Corran Cake" (Lancashire for currant cake), so that rude lads — and I'm afraid some of the girls too on occasion — used to speak of her as "Edie Corran".

She and her family were regular worshippers at the neighbouring Baptist Chapel, where the adherents were often referred to disrespectfully by certain non-Baptists as "dippers".

One day, a few weeks before the 'drawers' episode, one of the girls arrived at school with exciting news: "Edie Corran's going to be dipped on Sunday", she declared. Four or five decided on the spot that they were going to the service. I myself was attending the Baptist Sunday School at the time. My grandparents had been prominent members of the congregation, my aunt had played the organ at the Chapel and my parents had been married there. For all these reasons I felt that I had a prior right to sit in the front pew of the gallery. We were anxious not to miss any part of the spectacle. We had all heard tales — quite untrue of course! — of the minister letting girls slip as he lowered them into the water. I must confess that we were hoping for some such mishap to occur on this occasion. The tank containing the water was located in front of the pulpit and had two or three steps leading down. Normally it was kept covered with carpeting etc. I don't remember ever being present when a male was baptised, so to this day I don't know what the men wore. A young lady, however, always wore a white dress and her mother or an older friend would wait inside the Communion rails holding a large white towel. When the girl came out of the water all dripping wet, her mother would wrap the towel round her and lead her into the vestry.

This, then, was what we went to see, and if any of the four or five young girls present had been praying, I'm afraid their petition would have taken the form of a plea to the Almighty to allow the minister to "let Edie Corran slip back into the water". I don't believe we would have gone so far as to ask Him to let her drown...but I'm not sure. Anyway, after the 'drawers' episode I felt some contrition. Perhaps I had misunderstood her; she must be kinder than I had thought. Was it her Baptism that had brought about a change in her? Well, I never did find out. But we certainly drew some satisfaction from seeing her dripping wet from head to foot as she was helped out of the water. I suppose that was really as much as we could hope for.

Chapter 4

Orders To View

Another little girl with whom I used to play lived in the next street; her name was Alice Brown and, though far smaller than I, she was actually two years older. She was the youngest in her family and to me all her brothers and sisters seemed like adults. They all worked in the cotton mills but of course Alice was still at school. She was a quiet, friendly child and, unlike the rest of us, who occasionally fell out with one another, she never seemed to quarrel with the other girls. She had more aunts, uncles and cousins than I had ever heard of; by comparison I used to feel somewhat deprived. All my relatives (except, of course, those at home) lived at Southport and at that time I had only three cousins. Alice, on the other hand, seemed to have cousins in almost every street around us.

I think I must have been about seven years old when Alice came round one day to tell me that her grandmother had died. In those days I knew nothing of death, so the information made no impression on me; it meant nothing. She asked me if I would like to look at her grandma, and this seemed a perfectly normal thing to do. Without hesitation I agreed and off we went to her grandma's house nearby. As I reflect upon it now, I feel that to allow two children to enter that room to see an old lady in her coffin was decidedly strange; yet no one seemed to take the slightest notice of us. Most children, you might suppose, would have been scared; we, however, were quite unmoved. Indeed, as I look back I seem to remember that in some strange way we quite enjoyed the experience — so much so that for several weeks following it became something of a habit with us to view the dead. Alice would come round to say that so-and-so had died; should we go to look at him or her, as the case might be. Needless to say, we never mentioned these visits to my mother. I suppose she imagined we were just out playing hopscotch etc.

We next viewed two children, both of whom Alice had known personally. The first was a girl who had always been slightly mental and had been known to us as 'Silly Nellie' (Aren't children cruel sometimes!). Her mother, poor thing, seemed pathetically grateful and touched that two little girls should want to see Nellie in her coffin. There she was, all in white, with an arum lily in her hand. We thought this quite beautiful — so different from the old lady — and made all the appropriate noises. "Can you sing 'Jesus loves me'?" asked her mother, "Nellie used to sing that." Accordingly, ever ready to show our sympathy and make ourselves useful, we sang one verse of the hymn. I truly believe that Nellie's mother was deeply moved.

The next dead child we went to see was a little boy of only two years old. Again the mother seemed pleased to find that two little girls cared about her baby. It might seem that we were stony hearted; our true attitude, however, could be described as 'sympathy mingled with enjoyment'.

As I have said, Alice always knew the people we went to see; I suppose she obtained her information from her grown-up family. One day she came to the door saying: "Mrs Naesmith has died; shall we go and see her?" Yes, of course we'd go, we agreed. However, when we knocked at the door it was to find Mr Naesmith, a brawny Scotsman, glaring down at us. "Please can we look at Mrs Naesmith?" asked Alice quite politely. He looked astounded and outraged, as well he might. "NO YOU CANNOT!" he barked in angry tones, and he shut the door in our faces. We considered this a dreadful way to treat two little girls who had nothing but the kindest of thoughts and intentions towards bereaved relatives. As I say, we had not mentioned anything of our macabre visits to my mother hitherto, but so disappointed and disgusted were we at Mr Naesmith's brusque dismissal of us that I told her all about it, no doubt expecting some sympathy. Then of course the entire story of our 'viewings' came out. To say that my mother was shocked and appalled would be putting it mildly. She was utterly horrified — so much so that I really believe she began to wonder what sort of monster her eldest child was turning into, so young and so untender! Needless to say, that was the end of that kind of entertainment for us. What peculiar children we must have been!

We were out playing one Saturday morning when Alice remarked: "Our Maggie's getting married this afternoon." This was interesting; I was every bit as ignorant about weddings as about funerals. "Will you be going?" I asked, feeling sure that she would. However, her reply was: "No, I'm not going to the wedding but I am going to the 'do' afterwards. You can come too if you want." Ever the opportunist, I jumped at the chance. What a 'do' was I hadn't the faintest idea; I'd never heard of such a thing before, but Alice had a knowledge of the grown-up world which had not yet been imparted to me; anything she suggested was sure to be exciting and an improvement on hopscotch, which seemed to be the only alternative that particular day.

Accordingly, that afternoon Alice and I walked down the main road until we came to a very short street with a mill on one side and about six small cottages on the other. These opened straight onto the pavement and when we reached the third house the door stood open and the room within seemed full of people — so full that it seemed improbable that we would ever be able to squeeze ourselves in. But of course we did; we were never lacking in determination.

Among all the grown-ups there we saw one boy who looked about twelve years old. As we fought our way in he was entertaining the company by wriggling in and out of the spindles and back rails of a chair. Underneath and over the top he went, a real contortionist; it would have been easy to believe that he had no bones in his body. He won warm applause and the men present made a collection and gave him a lot of pennies. I was fascinated. I had never seen anything like this before and I thought I might try something remotely approaching his skills when I got home. However, common sense prevailed as I reflected that there was considerably more of me than of the 'boy wonder'!

No further memories of that afternoon have survived, but I believe someone must have told me that it was time to go home for tea. At all events, I found myself walking in that direction, though this time without Alice. "Where have you been?" asked my mother, the usual question as I arrived home. "I've been to a 'do' with Alice Brown," I proudly answered. "A WHAT?" shouted my mother. "I've been to a 'do'," I reiterated. Full explanations followed and by this time even I could see the shocked amazement on my mother's face. She warned me what dire punishment would follow if I went anywhere like that again without permission. For my part I was no less surprised than she — surprised at the 'unreasonableness' of parents. I couldn't understand it. Didn't they want their children to have any enjoyment? Well at any rate, Alice Brown could always be relied upon to come up with something unusual, even if it was only the enlargement of my vocabulary. She was such a NICE little girl!

15

Chapter 5

A Child's Heaven

Many people cannot accept that 'heaven' and 'hell' are the fanciful places we were taught about as children. No mansions in the sky with angels playing harps; no awful pits of everlasting fire where Satan pokes about with a huge toasting fork! Heaven and hell, such people maintain, represent states of mind which we live through during our earthly existence. If this is true, then in the course of my long life I have known both states.

From the time of my earliest memories heaven for me was spelt 'SOUTHPORT'. It was there that my grandparents and my much loved Auntie Maud had their home. As I was the eldest child in our family, I went there more often than any of my brothers and sisters. My earliest visits were probably timed to coincide with another addition to the family; I was sent there to be out of the way. On those golden days my mother would bathe me, wash my hair and dress me in my best clothes, ready for Grandpa to take me to Southport. How well I remember one occasion! I had been rigged out with a new coat and boots. My coat was red and I took great pleasure in it, but the delight of my life was to gaze at my new boots. They were black with white buttons and buttonholes stitched with white. Never before had I had a pair of boots like them; boots which actually came up my legs. My usual wear was black slippers with straps across the ankles.

To busy mothers, buttoned boots of that sort must have been a major nuisance. Our small fingers were incapable of manipulating the button-hook, that essential tool, so as to pull the buttons through the holes. Sometimes the button-hook would be missing. Many a time the buttons would come off or even be lost altogether. Then it would be a case of finding a spare one and stitching it on. All in all, what a trial those boots must have been!

A CHILD'S HEAVEN

Once washed and dressed, I would be sent across the road to the mill where Mr Loud, the watchman, would emerge to take me to Grandpa's office. If Grandpa himself was not in, I would be lifted onto one of the high office chairs and told to wait. Waiting, of course, was agony but what else could I do? I suspect now that I was always sent off too early — it wouldn't have done to keep Grandpa waiting; anyway, it was never too soon for me. When at last he came in, Grandpa would spend a few minutes (though to me it seemed like hours; didn't he realise that the train might go without us?) pottering about the office until at last he was ready. Then off we would go, walking down Union Road to Church Station, then up a long flight of steps to the platform.

Once the train had come steaming into the station, Mr Greenhalgh, the station master, would open a carriage door and in we would get. I always wondered how Grandpa knew it was the right train. The seats would be covered with horsehair upholstery which was decidedly scratchy to my bare parts, but that was a mere detail, happily ignored. How I loved that train ride! To this day I have still not outgrown my liking for train journeys, even though nowadays they are so different. I would sit contentedly looking out of the window until we left Preston. After Preston I'm afraid I used to pester Grandpa somewhat, asking him as we passed each station: "How many more stations before we get to Southport?" He never seemed to mind and would tell me the number before returning to his paper.

Then at last...St Luke's, the Southport suburb! By the time we had got out and started to walk I would be almost dancing with excitement. Down Tithebarn Road we would march and into Sussex Road. This was a wide and pleasant road with trees on either side and trams running up and down between Blowick and town. It was considered what the house agents of today would describe as "a desirable and select neighbourhood". The houses had long gardens back and front, and it seemed as though they were always filled with wallflowers. Long after I was grown-up the smell of wallflowers would waft my memory back to Sussex Road. (How is it that nowadays they have so much less scent?)

At last we would arrive at 'Ivy Dene' and Grandpa would let me run up the garden path to ring the bell at the front door. To me this was no ordinary door. It opened in the middle letting you into a vestibule with a further door beyond. Such front doors were known as 'storm doors' and when they were opened they revealed a step which I thought of as a 'gold' step. When I became older and went to school, this 'gold' step was one of the things I used to brag about. Of course I have long been aware that 'all is not gold that glitters', and that Auntie Maud used to have to keep that step bright and shiny with metal polish. Yet to me in those days that step was made of pure gold. Moreover, I was sure that no one else had one.

17

Everything in Southport was so different from Oswaldtwistle. At Oswaldtwistle, instead of flags, the footpaths were paved with blue-grey quarry tiles. Again at Oswaldtwistle we had only a smallish front garden and no back one at all. Until I was eight years old we had no bathroom either. Grandma, on the other hand, had a splendid one with a broad wooden ledge running round the top. On this I would sit watching her while she had a wash prior to taking me out in the afternoon. In that bathroom scented soap was always on hand — another amenity which we did not enjoy at home. Everything was so different and, so far as I was concerned, so much better.

On the walls of the dining and drawing rooms, near the fireplaces, handles were provided and if you turned them bells would ring in the kitchen. In the kitchen itself a whole row of these bells could be seen with letters underneath to show which rooms they were connected with. When one of the handles was pulled in the room concerned, the appropriate bell swayed on its wire. Sadly I was forbidden to play with these handles, fascinating though they were. Beside each of them stood a little glass tube covered with crotchet and holding tapers. Of course there was no electricity and when I was put to bed I was allowed to carry one of these tapers lighted, with Auntie walking beside me to see that I didn't set anything on fire. Sometimes the tapers would be coloured and I considered this the height of elegance.

About once a week Grandma would take me to town. I have had many delightful holidays in my life, but none ever gave me greater happiness than those trips to town with Grandma. We would catch a tram just outside the gate (this in itself was a great treat!) and Grandma always gave me the money to pay the conductor. It seemed to be the same conductor every time we went and he always said: "Ah, you're taking Grannie out again, are you?" Once we arrived in town, we would make our way to various shops, chiefly, I think, to buy food. Occasionally, however, we would go to Ramsbottom's, a large draper's shop. Since our usual purpose in visiting it was for Grandma to buy something for me to wear, of all the shops Ramsbottom's was my special delight. I particularly remember a pale blue woollen dress and the distinctive smell it bore.

Yet quite apart from any purchase on my behalf, there was the joy and wonder of the wooden balls which ran along wires after the assistant had unscrewed one and put the money and the bill in. Then she would pull a handle and round the shop it would travel above our heads. A lady in a sort of cage would take it out, put the change in it, and send it back to the counter where the assistant would be waiting to give the change back to Grandma. To me it was pure magic. None of our shops at

Oswaldtwistle could boast such sophisticated equipment. What child today can derive such enjoyment from a 'checkout' in a superstore?

When we returned to Ivy Dene I was always puzzled to discover that we were on the other side of the road, so that we had to cross over to Grandma's house. Strange — for had we not caught the tram on the side where the house stood? Silly child that I was, it was years before I could fathom that out.

At dinner time on Saturdays Grandpa would go down to the cellar and bring up a bottle of wine. 'Hock', he told me it was called, and I looked forward to the time when he would carefully remove the gold foil round the cork. At that point he would give me a penny. I would wrap the foil round the penny and gently smooth it until the penny showed through. I believe the process probably kept me quiet and occupied for an hour or so.

In the back garden stood apple, pear and cherry trees, and it included a smaller patch for lettuce, onions, radishes etc. To me it was a veritable Garden of Eden. As the years went by, the size of the garden visibly shrank each time I visited it — or so it seemed. As one grows older this experience is multiplied many times over, as in the well-known case of policemen getting younger and younger. Now, however, I am writing of the days when I was very young and what it felt like to be alive then. I have an excellent 'long' memory, though yesterday's events do not always spring so readily to mind. This is what is involved in 'growing old'.

Chapter 6

For What We Are About To Receive

Another of the girls with whom I used to play lived just oppposite to us; her name was Bessie and she was about a year older than I. She was quite good looking with dark, curly hair. It filled me with unreasonable envy, for my own hair was quite devoid of curls and needed to be plaited every night. Since she was the only girl in the family, her parents doted on her. She had four brothers, two older and two younger than herself.

One day her mother came across to ask mine if I could go with Bessie to Wilpshire the following day. Bessie seemed to have a number of better-off relations scattered round the district, and she called them all 'Auntie'. One such 'aunt', a Mrs Knowles, had two daughters several years older than Bessie and as they grew out of their clothes, a parcel was periodically made up to be passed on to Bessie herself. Now Mrs Knowles had written to say that just such a parcel was waiting to be picked up and inviting Bessie to come over to Wilpshire for it. Thus it was arranged that we should both go.

Now to two girls of our age — I suppose we would have been eight or nine — a journey to Wilpshire was quite an undertaking. To catch the tram to Blackburn we had to walk more than a mile. From that tram we had to change to another which would take us to Wilpshire itself. Of course Bessie had already made the journey with her mother several times, so she acted as guide.

Eventually we arrived, to be met at the door by Mrs Knowles, who conducted us into the kitchen-living room. Here one of her daughters was on her knees polishing the lino with milk! Now in the course of the journey Bessie had primed me well on the well-to-do state of the Knowles, and the sight of a young lady polishing the floor in such a way seemed to confirm all that she had told me. Surely they must be well off indeed if they could afford to use milk for polishing floors! To me this was a wholly novel idea and I was deeply impressed.

When dinner time came Mr Knowles came home from the mill where he was manager and we all sat down to table, a parent at either end, the two daughters on one side, and Bessie and myself on the other. As usual we were hungry and looking forward to the meal when suddenly thunder and lightning struck us with a vengeance and from a quite unexpected quarter, or so it seemed to Bessie and me. "Bessie," said Mr Knowles, "will you say grace?" Bessie stared in stupefaction, went a dull red and seemed to be gasping for air. As for me, my blood had turned to ice; that is what it felt like as I anguished with and for Bessie, fearing that once they realised that she had lost all power of speech, I would be the next one to be asked. Fortunately, kindly Mrs Knowles realised Bessie's embarrassment. "Who says it at home, Bessie?" she enquired. "Our Fred," stammered Bessie without a moment's hesitation. I stared at her in utter amazement. Fred! He was Bessie's eldest brother and anyone less likely to say grace I could not imagine. Had he lived in the present age, Fred would have been a 'punk rocker'. By this time the crisis was looming ever larger; I felt that my turn was coming any minute. Oh to be back at Oswaldtwistle! However, at this point, probably feeling that his dinner had been long enough delayed, Mr K. took over, quickly mumbling the necessary words without further ado. Bessie and I felt our breathing return to normal — well, almost normal; we had had a major shock.

What we ate at that meal I don't now remember but I'm sure we did it full justice. Needless to relate, the saying of grace was not an everyday custom in most of the homes in our district, and certainly not in our house. On the rare occasions when the minister came to tea I suppose he would be invited to 'ask a blessing' (that was the accepted phrase), whereupon we would close our eyes in embarrassed silence while he uttered the appropriate words. Certainly, however, it was not done in the ordinary way in our society. We all attended Sunday School and Chapel regularly, but saying 'grace before meat' was another matter.

After dinner Mr K. asked us what we would like to do in the afternoon. At that time roller-skating was just becoming popular and Bessie, with all the assurance of a Cook's Tour courier, immediately replied that we were going to Copster Green where there was an open-air skating rink. Copster Green was a small hamlet about half a mile away and was a favourite picnic place for Children's Sunday School outings. Apart from the skating rink it possessed few attractions except for swings, see-saws etc., but several cottages did have notices in their windows saying: "Teas: Boiled eggs, Tea and Bread and Butter — Price 9d. With Jam — Price 1/-.

Off we went, therefore, along the country road, which in those days was little more than a lane. Of course there were no cars whatever and in fact we never saw any vehicles at all; neither did we see any people until we reached Copster Green itself. We had not gone far, however, before the fertility of Bessie's brain began to make itself felt. Among the other girls with whom we played at home she was known as a bit of a 'lie-teller'. I think she herself almost believed the exaggerated tales she sometimes told. On this occasion, therefore, when she suddenly looked round and said: "I think there's someone following us," I was neither unduly surprised nor perturbed. A month or two before, a girl had been murdered in Accrington and of course all the papers had been full of it. To Bessie such horrors were meat and drink, and for some time all strange men were 'throat-cutters'. Needless to say, on this occasion we were not being followed.

Eventually we came to the first cottages and just as we were about to pass, Bessie stopped and exclaimed: "I know the lady who lives here. She's a friend of my mother's — we'd better call; she'd expect us to. I had my doubts; to me it seemed somewhat unecessary, but by this time Bessie had already marched up to the door and knocked. The lady who opened the door seemed a little surprised to see two children but recognised Bessie and asked us in. She enquired about Bessie's mother and family and wanted to know what we were doing so far from home. Bessie explained everything and added that we were going to find the skating rink. "Oh," said the lady, "and are you coming back for tea?" Obviously she had received quite the wrong impression of our means, but Bessie quickly replied: "Oh yes, and we'll have the same as we had when I came here with Mother." "Ham and eggs?" asked the lady in great surprise, "That will be 1/6d each." I stood up in stunned silence; Bessie had surpassed herself. As we walked away from the house I felt like running back to Wilpshire! "Whatever did you say that for?" I exclaimed as soon as we were out of earshot and I had recovered my speech. "You know we're going back to your auntie's for tea and you also know that we've only got 6d each." Bessie merely shrugged. "Oh well," she said, "I didn't like to say no. I think she expected us back for tea."

We found the so-called 'skating rink', which turned out to be the flat roof of a bungalow. The man who came to the door said that it would cost us 6d. each but Bessie said that we only had 6d. between us. "All right," he said finally, "You can have half an hour for the 6d." The money proved to be ill spent. The surface of the 'rink' was cracked concrete and the skates he lent us did not fit. However we stayed until he came to tell us that our time was up. We thought him a most unchristian man to treat two 'young ladies' like that. Altogether it was rather disappointing.

FOR WHAT WE ARE ABOUT TO RECEIVE

We set out to return to Wilpshire, almost running past the cottage where Bessie had so grandly ordered ham and eggs. Naturally when we got back this episode was not mentioned to Mrs K., and I don't suppose that Bessie told her mother about calling on her friend.

As we walked along, the topic of 'grace' became once more of prime importance. Whatever should we say if either of us was asked to say grace at tea-time? The only form of grace we could think of was the verse we sang every morning at school before going home for dinner: "Be present at our table Lord", etc. Just one line didn't seem quite adequate; on the other hand a whole verse seemed too long — a bit much, we felt, for a private house. As we reached the house our problem was still unsolved, so we were forced to leave matters to sort themselves out. Fortunately for our peace of mind, there was no mention of grace at tea-time. Perhaps once a day was considered enough to cover all meals. At all events, we were profoundly relieved!

When tea was over, we put on our hats and coats again; it was time to set off for home. Bessie was given the parcel of clothes and in addition, as Mrs K. was seeing us off at the door, she gave Bessie a shilling, telling her that it was to be divided among her brothers on her return. Now Bessie had confidently expected her 'auntie' to speed the parting guests with largess of some kind — indeed, in view of the fact that we had spent our money on the skating rink, we were both relying on it heavily. Thus the shilling did not come up to our expectations — especially as it was to be divided among four undeserving brothers. The first priority was our return fares to Oswaldtwistle — on that we were both agreed. By the time Bessie arrived home, therefore, I don't suppose there was much, if anything of the shilling left to be distributed. Somehow I think it would never have been mentioned. It would have remained as chimerical as "our Fred's grace". In the unlikely event of being questioned about it, Bessie would always find the appropriate answer. She was that sort of girl.

Chapter 7

Holidays — Crossing t'Watter

It was the custom for all the Lancashire mill towns to have their annual summer holidays at set times, each town having its own week. During that week all the factories in the town concerned would close down and most of the shops closed as well. In those days there was no holiday pay and the saying was that people who were going away always left a week's wage 'under the clock' for when they came home. At that time three pounds was a very good wage for a man, while the women weavers usually earned about twenty-five shillings a week. Most mills ran a holiday club and the workers, women in particular, would pay in a shilling or two when they drew their wages. For people in Oswaldtwistle the favourite holiday resort was probably Blackpool, with Southport, Morecambe or Fleetwood as alternatives. Any one of these resorts was very easy to reach. There was always a good train service, and for the Holiday Week specials were laid on. Many people booked their lodgings from one year to another, the same house, the same bedroom, the same landlady. There was very little 'boarding' at that time; people used to take most of their food with them and the landlady would cook whatever was given her each day. Terms were so much a night per bed — usually about two shillings, and there were generally two or three beds in a room. It was quite common for several strangers to be accommodated in the same room. Of course there were always some people who could afford to get off their work for an extra day or two, and they would go even further afield. They were considered extremely lucky, being able to manage ten days holiday, sometimes to places as far away as Llandudno or even Torquay.

Plenty of people, however, never got away at all. We ourselves never went away during Holiday Week. I remember one year on the first Saturday of Holiday Week several of us children were clustered round the doorway of a house eagerly listening while a boy who lived there (he was a few years older than most of us) held forth about the holiday on which he was about to embark. Normally he would have been entirely ignored but this particular morning he had to have an audience, for was he not going to a far-away place called "T'Isle o' Man?" Although I had never seen him properly dressed before, there he was, dressed and ready to set off at any minute. The tales he was telling about his journey to this unknown place — his voyage, one would almost be justified in calling it — were far-fetched in the extreme. After some time one of the lads who was listening exclaimed: "Nay Bill, I think th'art stretching it a bit aren't ta?" For a few seconds Bill stopped speaking. Then he said solemnly: "Stretching it? D'you think I'd tell a lie before I'm going o'er t'watter?" A pregnant silence followed. We all felt the seriousness of the situation. Of course he would never tell a lie before going into such danger. No explorer ever ventured forth into unknown lands with greater seriousness or more bravery. Bill Driver was contemplating his first crossing of 't'watter'. For fifty-one weeks of the year he was a rather uncouth sort of lad, somewhat beneath our notice. Now, however, as we gazed at him with awe, he had assumed heroic qualities.

I believe that must have been the first time I had ever heard of the Isle of Man. Years later, when I was learning dressmaking, a lady came into the shop the week before the Holidays. "Are you going away next week, Mrs Barker?" asked Mrs May. "No," she replied, "but our David's going t'Isle o' Man." "Oh," said Mrs May, "is he going to Douglas?" "No," insisted Mrs B., "I've told you — he's going t'Isle o' Man." Which seems to point to the fact that even at that time it was not a very well known resort — not in Oswaldtwistle at any rate!

On a later occasion Tom's brother Joe was taking his lady friend to spend a few days in Douglas. Sally had not been on a ship before and after they had been sailing for about an hour she began to feel a little queasy. Declaring that she was going to the ladies' toilets, she set off leaving Joe at the top of the steps. After waiting for some time and seeing no sign of Sally returning, he went to the bar and bought a glass of whisky. Then, waylaying a stewardess who was just about to go down the steps, he asked her to give the whisky to a Miss Taylor who was not feeling too well. She assured him that she would do her best to find his friend and see that she was all right. Before long Sally herself came up the steps looking much better. "My word, Joe," she exclaimed, "they don't half look after you on this ship! One of the stewardesses is going round with glasses of whisky for anyone who isn't feeling well — and she knew my name too. I call that marvellous service." So much for crossing t'watter!

For two or three years my father rented a cottage in Downham for three or four weeks in the summer. We children enjoyed every minute of these holidays. I remember how, at various times, groups of people would come to Downham in horse-drawn charabancs. I should think they were chiefly choir picnics and they always congregated on the bridge to sing. So universal was this custom that for many years I firmly believed that they were not allowed to come any further than the bridge until they had sung the hymn, "When the roll is called up yonder". They always seemed to sing that. One year Aunt Emily came for a few days and having a fit of economising on my mother's behalf, she sent us older children out to pick nettles which she was going to boil as a second vegetable for our evening meal. We didn't think much of the idea at all, particularly when it started to rain as we picked the stinging leaves. We had been assured that if we grasped them firmly the nettles wouldn't sting, but either the nettles themselves had not been told or else we were not grasping them firmly enough. When the time came for us to eat the resulting green mess, none of us liked it. Afterwards Mother often told us that when Auntie had boiled the nettles and chopped them up, she used more butter etc. than the dish was worth. Well, I suppose her intentions were good even if the nettles were not!

The cottage we stayed in had a room upstairs running the length of the entire building and also of the one next door. It had a flagged floor and had originally been used to house a weaving loom. It made an ideal playroom on rainy days, but if we became too boisterous or energetic the old lady who lived next door used to come and complain that we were shaking the ornaments off her mantlepiece. She frightened us by saying that the floor might collapse if we jumped about on it too much.

We were friendly with a little girl who lived on the next farm and together we would spend hours searching in the hedges for wild strawberries. Her mother would then give us each a cup of milk with a spoonful of sugar in it into which our strawberries would go to be eaten with a spoon. Those berries were invariably unripe and almost tasteless, but to us they were the greatest treat. Half the pleasure consisted in looking for and finding them.

One of the village cottages was minute: it had just one room which opened straight out into the road. It was inhabited by an old woman who kept her bed at the back of the single room, while on the table in the window stood boxes and bottles of sweets etc. Just inside the door stood a second table on which the scales were kept. Whenever we had a copper to spend we always went there because the old lady would let us serve ourselves. How we loved to weigh the sweets and how anxious and careful we were to be 'just'! We would almost have cut a jelly baby in two rather than give ourselves overweight. I don't think this was because we were all that scrupulously honest. Rather it was because we so much enjoyed this bit of real shopkeeping that we felt it might come to an end if we were not extra strict in giving fair measure. I often wonder how much pleasure the old lady derived from watching our efforts to weigh a ha'porth of sweets with such meticulous care.

Once a week a neighbouring farmer used to kill a pig or a sheep and we would stand round the slaughterhouse door watching the men cutting up the carcases and washing everything down. No, the sight never worried us in the least, nor did it make vegetarians of us. It was just another entertainment which was only to be found in the country and we took it all for granted. Every day we used to fetch the milk from the farm and I believe it was no more than tuppence or threepence a quart. It would be warm — straight from the cow, and we loved it.

Chapter 8

New Year's Day

As celebrated in Oswaldtwistle, New Year's Day used to be a very busy and exciting occasion. In the morning all the Sunday Schools had 'coffee and bun'. The children had to take their own mugs for the coffee and practically everyone would take a special presentation mug commemorating some former coronation or jubilee. Such mugs were generally stored away in a cupboard or display cabinet and used only for 'coffee and bun' at Sunday School.

At our house the coronation mugs never seemed to last as long as at other people's. I cannot believe they were more brittle than those of my friends but if a prize had been offered for breaking crockery, we as a family would, I am sure, have won it. Coronation mugs simply could not keep pace with our depredations, with the result that more often than not we were compelled to take ordinary cups. This we felt as something of a let-down, a disappointment, and I used to find myself wondering why we couldn't save things like other families. However, it never spoiled my enjoyment for long.

By about ten or ten-thirty in the morning, when we would arrive at Sunday School, the whole place would be bathed in an atmosphere of happiness and good humour and pervaded by the warm, welcoming smell of coffee, buns and oranges. "Happy New Year!" everyone would be calling. The coffee was invariably in Mr May's charge and he would be seated on a chair beside the kitchen door. In front of him would be a very large bread mug filled with the steaming brew, and as each scholar proffered his or her mug he would dip a jug into the bread mug and pour the coffee in. Meanwhile the teachers would be collecting the buns from the kitchen and distributing them to the scholars — quite large and substantial buns too; either currant or seed buns could be chosen. So substantial were they that apart from a few of the bigger boys, no one, I think, could manage to eat an entire bun at a sitting.

Most of us would carry a good portion of our bun home with us together with an orange. The latter, I remember, were invariably small and very sour.

Usually, before we left for home some of the younger girls would go to the vestry to practise a 'Dialogue'. The word ought to be written in capital letters, so large and important did it loom in our imaginations. It consisted of a little playlet, and was considered the star turn of the entertainment always provided by the choir and Sunday School scholars. We used to fancy ourselves prodigiously in our roles.

After a practise we would return home to a scrappy lunch — no cooking on New Year's Day! — and then prepare for the rest of the day's activities. If we were lucky (and we generally were) we would meet the Oswaldtwistle Silver Band coming up the lane, for this was their day for going round the town playing at various points and collecting money from the houses nearby. The quality of their playing was never more than mediocre, but the way in which they collected their funds really amounted to a sort of refined blackmail. First they would play some short piece, then one or two of the men would knock on the doors hoping to collect money from the residents. After that they would play a second piece and the length of this would depend on the amount collected after the first. The more the coppers, the longer the piece. It was these New Year occasions that used to evoke the first intimations of snobbishness in my character. Because my father had contributed half-a-crown, the band would play "A Fine Old English Gentleman" (one of the top ten in their repertoire) in front of our house. When they played that particular piece everyone would know that the householder had 'coughed up' to the tune of two and six. Not many, I believe, were so generous, and my vain little ego used to swell with pride and satisfaction. Like the Pharisee in the parable, I was glad that we were different from others. (Pride comes before a fall!).

The tea-party in the afternoon was one of the great Sunday School events of the year. Three long tables were set up and members of the young ladies' class considered it an honour to be asked to 'have a table'. Two ladies would be in charge of each table and they would bring their own knives and teaspoons, around which they would have tied coloured thread in order to be able to claim their own when the party was over. They would also bring fancy table-centres and d'oyleys, cake-stands, cruets and tins of mustard, for many of the men demanded mustard for the ham sandwiches.

Between these table ladies there would be a certain amount of friendly competition as to whose table was the most attractive. To supplement their own efforts they used to need what were known as 'back-waiters', and for this they would recruit girls of about twelve to fourteen. To be asked to be a 'back-waiter' was an honour indeed. 'Back-waiting' meant walking along behind the diners and picking up cups to be refilled. You would take them to the head of the table where the tea ladies presided and then hurry back with the filled cups. You also had to keep an eye on the plates of sandwiches (ham, beef and tongue), and if one was becoming empty you raced to the kitchen, where members of the 'Mothers' Class' were sitting at a long table cutting and buttering bread. At the same time one or two of the men would be carving the meat, while yet other ladies would be marrying it with the bread and butter, thereby giving birth to a fresh plate of sandwiches. After exchanging your empty plate for one of these full ones, you would speed back to the table. Then you would probably start on the cake-stands. Much to the disgust of many of the participants, one particular woman was always in charge of the cake in the kitchen. So niggardly was she that you might have thought that she personally and alone had provided all that cake. The pieces she cut were so small that most people would take two at a time, thereby frustrating A.A.'s scheme to make the cake go a long way. She really did begrudge giving out that cake — especially when the young men got to the table. When they saw the size of the pieces they were quite outspoken about it, and at that particular table the back-waiters were kept extra busy refilling the cake-stands.

When everyone had eaten as much as they wanted, they would leave the table and go and sit in the chapel. Here yet more people would be patiently waiting for the tables to be re-set. In the schoolroom everyone would be scurrying round like demented rabbits, and again the tables would compete with one another as to which could be first to be ready for the second sitting. This was followed by a third sitting when the whole procedure was re-enacted. Then, with everyone replete and content, all would transfer themselves to the chapel to wait for the entertainment to take place. Old friends and scholars would be chatting among themselves and everyone would be looking happy to be greeting another year in this particular time-honoured way and in these familiar surroundings.

One young man in particular stands out in my memory. Though not a 'native' of the village, he was a relative of the Sunday School superintendent and always used to come to the New Year's party. As an individual he was thin and ill-looking with a dead-white face, and he ate as though for weeks on end he had never had a bite. In fact it was some time before anyone discovered that he was in the habit of getting through all three sittings! How he managed it I don't know, for tickets were always collected at the tables. Perhaps someone felt sorry for him — he might have been considered "a bit weak in t'head". Poor man, he died before he was forty.

In the meantime the schoolroom would be a scene of hectic activity. All the workers would have combined forces to clear the tables, collect the cutlery etc. — and all in the shortest possible time. Round the pulpit and resting on the

30

communion rails a platform would have been erected and the piano would have been lifted into place on it so that everything was ready for the Grand Concert. After a prayer and some opening remarks by the chairman, the first item was always a glee by the choir. This would often be followed by a recitation. Two young women in particular were regarded as top reciters, one being extremely dramatic, the other tending towards humorous Lancashire pieces. The burning ambition of all the 'artistes' was to be 'clapped on'; the word 'encore' was, I believe, quite unknown to us.

Then would come the Dialogue, and how we loved this part! There were usually parts for six or seven girls, and these would have been waiting in the vestry in trembling anticipation. In themselves those dialogues were trifling enough — slight little sketches which called for very little acting. That was just as well; more often than not, one or two of the girls would forget their lines and have to be prompted loudly by the teacher who had 'trained' them. It was usually A.A., the parsimonious distributor of cake. Yet however trivial or amateurish they might objectively speaking have been, the fact remains that everyone genuinely enjoyed them — though truth to tell, the players probably even more than the audience.

After the interval the choir would take over with glees, songs, duets etc., and occasionally a sketch. I recall one comic sketch called "A Trip to Blackpool". At the time I was a new member of the choir, but I was given a part in which all I had to say was: "I'm managing Peggy from Oldham". Though that is all I can now remember of the play, at the time it was considered hilariously funny and the applause was all that the choir could have desired — a fitting reward for their ιabour!

At last the concert came to an end. Everyone sang the doxology and then set off for home, feeling, no doubt, that they had started off another year in the recognised and proper manner. Now that we are eighty years on from those times, will today's young people have such happy memories of New Year's Day? I doubt it!

Chapter 9

Apprentice To Dressmaking

It was by sheer chance that I became an apprentice to dressmaking. Out shopping one day, my mother happened to enter the shop of a Mrs Bury. She remarked casually that her daughter Alice, who had just started business on her own, was needing an apprentice. Mother (an opportunist if ever there was one!) immediately declared that her daughter Florence, aged fourteen, would be glad to fill the vacancy. Never for one moment was the question raised whether I was suitable, or even whether I wanted to be a dressmaker. Mother said that I was able to use the sewing machine and that was that. I have often reflected how fortunate it was for me that it was not in the butcher's or the grocer's that my mother had chanced to hear of a vacancy. I might so easily have found myself apprenticed to sausage-making or butter-slapping!

Alice's sister, Mrs May, had a milliner's shop, and very soon after I had started working for Alice, the two sisters agreed that it would be an excellent idea for both businesses to have a joint workroom over Mrs May's shop. That, therefore, is where I spent my early working days. During my first year I was an apprentice and then, in my second, I was promoted to 'improver'. In the dressmaking world of that time I was considered lucky to be receiving two shillings and sixpence a week for my first year, for the system by which apprentices either paid a premium or worked for nothing was only just being discontinued by the larger firms. After that first year my wages were raised to the princely sum of 6/6d. per week.

In our small workroom we were a very happy little group. Mrs May had taken on an apprentice to millinery named Doris, and she and I were close friends for many years. She had a remarkable soprano voice and was taking lessons with a teacher from Manchester. In later years she became very well known in musical circles in

East Lancashire and I frequently acted as her accompanist, thereby basking in her reflected radiance. In any case it was a task I greatly enjoyed.

One of my first jobs as an apprentice was sewing hooks and eyes on the front linings of bodices (that was the name given to the top half of a dress). At that time all dresses had fitted linings and were equipped with whalebone strips stretched over the darts which were placed from waist to bustline. Dresses were almost floor length and the full skirts had brush-braid stitched just inside the hem to catch some of the dirt from the ground. This braid was about half an inch wide and one edge, which was left loose, had two or three rows of short plush fringe which was intended to sweep the floor, thereby saving the hems themselves. Hence the name 'brush-braid'.

Another task was sewing collar supports into the lace collars of dresses. They were made of thin wire bent into zigzags with loops at either end, and they could be stretched to fit any depth of collar. They were sewn inside the collar just below the ears, with one at the back to keep the collar from wrinkling. No dresses at that time (except, of course, for evening dresses) were collarless. I vividly remember the talk and to-do it caused when one of the local young ladies came back from a visit to London wearing a blouse with a V-neck. These blouses came to be known as 'pneumonia' blouses and it was supposed that doctors had condemned them as a danger to health. However, before long every young lady (and many not so young!) was wearing dresses without collars so that they exposed just a little of the chest. The new fashion provoked far more criticism in the daily papers than any topless dress of today can arouse on television or in the modern media.

Our normal working hours were nine to twelve-thirty, one to five-thirty and six p.m. to eight p.m. Sundays were, of course excepted, and on Wednesday work finished at one p.m. Our busiest times were in Spring and Summer. Each of the various churches and chapels had its own date for the Annual Anniversary, otherwise known as 'Sermons Sunday'. The first of these fell on the last Sunday in April, and the others followed on each in turn. Generally new clothes were bought only once a year, with perhaps a raincoat or winter coat every two years. If you were having new clothes, then 'Sermons Sunday' would be the occasion when you first wore them. All garments had to be finished and ready to be collected on the Saturday, and on a few occasions, when we were extra busy, we worked all of the previous Friday night.

Other days too could be especially busy — those on which we had a 'mourning order' in. When a member of a family died, it was the custom for the near relatives to go 'in mourning' — in other words to have new black clothes made for the funeral, for no one would have dreamt of going to a funeral in anything but black or

33

very dark clothes. When, therefore, we had a 'mourning order' in, it meant that we had only a few days in which to complete it and that would generally entail working overtime. I remember one occasion when a woman whose husband had just died brought in a black dress to have some crepe put on it. Alice gave me the job of stitching the 2-inch band of crepe round the bottom of the dress. When I had finished I was surprised and disappointed. Alice told me to take it all off; apparently I had put it on 'upside down'. I said that I didn't even know there was an 'up' and a 'down' to it. She then showed me that the plain-looking papery material had a small pattern on it like a water mark. This, she explained, represented tears. I had made the tear-drops fall upwards! I thought then — and I still do — that I had never heard of anything so silly. That was my only experience of crepe. Along with many other things, after the war it must have gone right out of fashion. In those days, however, it was the ultimate in the symbolism of mourning.

I seem to recollect that on the few occasions when we were allowed to work all night, Doris and I found it very exciting. Alice and Mrs May, however, used often to become extremely tired. On one such night Alice nodded off whilst sitting at the machine; her head actually came in contact with it! On another occasion, we had reached the early hours of the morning when Mrs May went off to lie on the fitting-room floor, declaring: "It doesn't matter — I'll have to have a few minutes' sleep. Wake me up in half an hour." Normally, however, they were very particular in ensuring that Doris and I were off the premises as soon as eight o'clock came. A workshop inspector began to call round rather frequently, and Alice seemed scared that he might find us still there after hours, even though we might only be standing there talking.

I think that that inspector must have enjoyed his visits to us, for he would sit by the fire (we used to have one from October to April), and I never knew him to make any sort of inspection of the premises etc. or ask any questions. All he did was to pin a large sheet of paper, the Factory Act, on the wall. That seemed to be the full extent of his intervention on our behalf. So accustomed did we become to him popping in, that after a time we used to tease him unmercifully, playing all kinds of tricks on him and pelting him with empty cotton reels as he went downstairs. Occasionally Mrs May would give him a cup of tea, but she didn't make a habit of it. I'm sure that he regarded his visits to Florence House (that was the name of the shop — nothing to do with me!) as a time of light relief from his usual factory visits.

Monday mornings were 'clearing up' mornings. Everything was put in its proper place, the table was cleared for the afternoon's cutting-out, the floor was swept and all the rag cuttings were put in an old orange box which lived under the table. The sweepings of the floor were sifted of all dropped pins and needles, which were then cleaned by rubbing them in tissue paper. The machine was cleaned, oiled and run in ready for use on Tuesday. Doris and I would take the box down the lane to the rag man, though he invariably said that he didn't want the cuttings; they were no use to him. Nevertheless, we always left them there and sauntered back with the empty box just in time for dinner!

Our workroom window happened to look out on the yard and garden of the pub next door. The landlord had recently died, so his widow and eldest son were carrying on the business. The son was one of the lazy sort and spent much time in the garden talking to a friend. The friend also gave the impression of having little work to do. They would stand there talking and staring into space until his mother's voice from inside would be heard calling: "Harry, Harry — t'bar!" After she had called a few times he would hurry inside. If Mrs May was downstairs in the shop we would sneak into a little back room where there was a window at right-angles to our workroom. When we saw Harry and his pal talking in the garden we would quietly open the window and: "Harry, Harry, t'bar!" we would call out in imitation of his mother. Our ruse worked for some time until he evidently began to think that something strange was going on. When next he saw us outside he gave us a decidedly surly look. "You — - milliners!" he said. Naturally we simply ignored him, but our little game was over. Nevertheless, it had been fun while it lasted. It didn't take much to amuse us in those days!

One day Doris came in with an exciting piece of news. It seemed that a friend of her father's had visited their shop. He had told the family that he was able to obtain a permit to see over the 'Mauretania'. She was lying in dock at Liverpool at the time, and was, I believe, the largest liner in the world then afloat. There and then Mrs May and Alice decided that we would have a 'works picnic' and everything was arranged for us to have the day off. The train journey to Liverpool was in itself a new and exciting experience, and after lunch we made our way to the docks where we met the man who had said he would take us on board this gorgeous ship.

Nowadays young people are habituated to seeing all kinds of wonders on television, but we at that time had only read about the 'Mauretania' in the papers. We had no idea whatever just how enormous such a ship was. When we stood on the top deck and looked down at the Mersey it seemed miles below us. It was like standing on the roof of a high block of flats. We were absolutely stupefied — there is no other word for it. I remember being shown into the library and thinking "It's larger than our town hall!"

Our next adventure was to take the ferry to New Brighton. The ferry — after the 'Mauretania', what a comedown! But at any rate none of us was seasick! Then we went to the Tower which, though nothing like the one at Blackpool, gave the impression of being very cosy, with a lot of people enjoying themselves. We spent half an hour there dancing and, much to Mrs May's disgust, Doris managed to lure two youths to dance with us. Mrs May really did take the responsibility of seeing that we behaved with the utmost seriousness. She was rather lacking in a sense of humour and in this respect was quite unlike her sister Alice, who was always ready for a lark. After having tea we returned to Liverpool to take the train for home. I have always felt glad that we were privileged actually to board the 'Mauretania'. It was the nearest thing to a cruise I ever attained!

Chapter 10

Sisters — We Were Seven

It is natural, I suppose, for girls who are 'only' children to wish that they had brothers and sisters. In my young days, however, I would willingly have changed places with any 'only' child, had that been possible. That I should quickly have rued the decision is more than likely, but, like most impossible dreams, at the time it seemed highly desirable. I hated being asked how many brothers and sisters I had. People seemed so amused when I told them, and I had the idea (quite mistakenly, I'm sure) that having a large brood of children had some kind of stigma attached to it.

Lucy Catlow was an 'only' child, and whenever I visited their house her mother never failed to ask me about the number of children we had. She invariably ended up by saying: "Our Lucy thinks you're very lucky. She wishes she had brothers and sisters like you!" Lucky? I thought I had never heard anything sillier. Anyway, I didn't believe it. How could any girl wish for more than Lucy had? The only child of a doting mother and father, with an uncle who was a salesman for a sweet firm! She always had an unlimited supply of chocolate and sweets, though come to think about it, I don't remember her ever passing any on to us, her playmates.

Then again, being the eldest did, I suppose, have some advantages, but there were so many drawbacks to weigh against them. As those sisters closest to me in age grew near to me in size, I had to keep a watchful eye on my clothes; it was all too easy for them to be quietly 'borrowed' for special occasions. The only articles of attire that were safe from predators were my shoes. They were invariably too large for any of the other girls in the family. One particular episode will always remain vivid in my mind. The 'Harvest' at the chapel was a very special day and in the course of the week before it I had made myself a new hat to grace the occasion. It was a purple toque with a large bow at the back and I was very proud of it. On the

Saturday night of that week Tom was taking me to the theatre in Accrington. So rare a treat was this that I thought seriously about wearing my new hat that evening. After great deliberations, however, I resolved to keep it for Sunday.

We had arrived at the theatre and were sitting in the stalls watching people coming in when suddenly I saw IT — my new hat, and on the head of my sister Annie! As she and her friend entered she caught my eye before quickly taking her seat a few rows in front of us. She must have been thinking what an unlucky chance it was that had brought us to the theatre that night, for we rarely went. What play we had gone to see I now have no idea. Whatever it was, so far as I was concerned I was too furious to care. In fact going to the theatre at all that night was a complete waste of Tom's hard-earned money. All I could think about was my beautiful hat having its initial outing on the head of my sister on a Saturday night and in a theatre — SACRILEGE!

I could mention many other occasions when my nicest things were 'borrowed', but I think the cheekiest was on my wedding-day. I had laid out all my special undies on my bed ready for the big moment when I should array myself in all my finery. Having so large a family meant that the one bathroom was occupied most of the morning. I was to be the last to use it, and when my turn came the water was barely tepid. By the time I was out of the bathroom everybody except my father had already left for the chapel. I started to dress and — what do you think? My knickers — my special white ones with the lace round the bottoms — had vanished, disappeared, GONE! I was forced to wear an ordinary pair! To this day I have never known for sure who it was who wore my bridal knickers. Though there were one or two whom I always suspected, they shall remain nameless. In the subsequent excitement of the wedding, honeymoon and move from the 'ancestral hall' the incident lost much of its importance, though it was never forgotten. Whoever the guilty one was, that time she got away with it (as well as the knickers!).

Another item of my wardrobe that I had to keep an eye open for was my hankies. I took to washing them myself so that I would always have a clean one when I needed it. Once they left my sight in the general wash, they seemed to disappear. At the time I am speaking of I was sleeping in one of the attic bedrooms, and a little way up the chimney I had discovered a small ledge just large enough to support a chocolate box. Here, then, was the perfect hiding place for my hankies. This surely was what turned me into a lifelong and obsessive hankie hoarder. One thing is certain. Even if I suffer from running colds for the rest of my days, I shall never run out of handkerchiefs!

Chapter 11

A Weekend in Bacup

It was some time in March 1913 that my father received a letter from the secretary of Zion Chapel, Bacup, inviting him to attend a Grand Re-opening. A new building had been added to the Chapel consisting of classrooms and vestries. There was to be a Dedication Service and all old scholars were being invited to attend. It was to be a weekend affair, starting on Saturday with lunch in the schoolroom. This was to be followed by a meeting in which the new building would formally be opened, after which there would be tea and then another evening meeting at which many of the stalwarts of the past would make speeches etc. On Sunday special services would be held all day. All in all, it was to be a marathon reunion.

When they lived in Bacup, my father's family had been zealous supporters of the Zion Chapel, but he himself had only been ten years old when they went to live at Southport. Hence his personal interest in the forthcoming celebrations was very mild indeed. On the other hand, my eldest aunt, who was living at Oswaldtwistle at the time, was considerably more moved by the letter; she had attended Zion until after she was married and went to live at Southport. Hence she retained a sentimental regard for Zion Chapel.

It was therefore decided that she and her daughter Gladys would attend and that I would go with them to represent my father. I must confess that my own interest in Zion was not much greater than my father's, but I was always ready to go to Bacup, where my half-cousin Arthur was an attraction and could be counted on for entertainment. However, I felt that my enjoyment would be enhanced if I could take my friend Doris with me, and after some correspondence with my father's Aunt Alice I was given permission to include Doris in the outing.

As I have already explained, in those days it was always the custom for us to wear our new Summer outfits for the first time on 'Sermons Sunday', whenever that happened to be. Our 'Sermons' at Stanhill was on the first Sunday in May, whereas the affair at Bacup was at the end of April. In view of the fact that the latter was to be so major and so auspicious an event, it was felt that an exception could be made; we could appear in our new clothes for the first time on that weekend.

It will be remembered that Doris and I were apprentices at the time, she to millinery and I to dressmaking. It was natural, therefore, that we should be very 'clothes conscious' and had almost begun to fancy ourselves as 'trend-setters' in Oswaldtwistle. We were always keen to have the very latest fashions (or what we thought were the latest!), and our bosses, I imagine, did nothing to discourage this. Whether they thought it might do something to advertise their business I don't know; viewed from this perspective, the idea does seem somewhat extravagant.

That year the latest thing was the military collar. It was made of stiff buckram and stood up round the neck leaving about six inches in front to be tied with ribbon. Doris' outfit was a costume of navy blue with a three-quarter-length coat which was pleated from the waist. The revers and collar were covered with silk in a pattern of Scotch plaid and she had a small hat made in the same material. Plaid ribbons to match were tied at the neck. As my brother had died the previous autumn, I was wearing 'half mourning'. It consisted of a purple coat with the new collar and a black velvet ribbon tie. I had a black tulle hat, almost like a lampshade, with ribbons also in black velvet. However, the very latest manifestations of our love of fashion were to be found on our legs — or rather, to be accurate, on our feet. That season had seen the start of the tango shoe. It was a kind of slipper, open at the instep and with lace-holes at either side. Ribbons were crossed over the instep and then — depending on how bravely fashionable you felt — crossed up the leg and tied with a bow at the top. Tango shoes were considered very daring. Doris' ribbons were in Scotch plaid to match those on her coat, while mine were black velvet. All in all, our tango shoes were in marked contrast to the more usual Gibson shoe.

Saturday was a normal working day for us, but on this occasion, of course, we had been excused. Accordingly, this special Saturday morning we proudly boarded a tram right in front of the shop. So conceited were we about our appearance that I really think we would not have considered a Lord Mayor's coach inappropriate for our journey. None being forthcoming, however, we had to make do with the only transport available to us.

To get to Bacup we had to change trams first at Accrington and then again at Haslingden. Soon after boarding the Haslingden tram we were horrified to see rain on the window and the further we went the harder it rained. This was truly a calamity of major proportions; neither of us had remembered to take an umbrella.

Whatever could we do? There we were with all our beautiful new clothes on, and the rain was pouring down! As the tram splashed its way into Bacup I had what I thought was a brainwave. Doris had never been to Bacup before, so she was not familiar with its geography. I, on the other hand, was a seasoned traveller on that line. "We'll get out at the station," I decided, "and get a cab up to Aunt Alice's, where we can borrow an umbrella to get to the Chapel." I should mention here that Father had given me the princely sum of a sovereign for collections etc. at the Chapel, but I felt that a cab-fare could safely be deducted as a legitimate expense. After all, a sovereign was a lot of money just to be given to a Chapel, and surely girls' new outfits were of primary importance!

At the station we got off the tram and made our way into the entrance hall. There was no one about except one man in the booking-office who looked as miserable as the weather outside. The sight of us ought to have brightened his outlook on life, but I'm afraid it merely confirmed his suspicions that his breakfast hadn't agreed with him and that he was 'seeing things'. After all, sights like ourselves could hardly have come into his view every day. "Are there no cabs about here?" I enquired in my best and most superior manner. He could not believe his ears! Two fancy 'chits' wanting a cab! "Did you want one?" he rejoined, swallowing several times. We assured him that a cab was indeed our dearest wish. He then said that he would 'phone for one and sure enough, before many more minutes had passed, a red-faced cabby stamped into the hall looking enquiringly at the booking-clerk. Strangely enough, he didn't see us at first. The clerk gave him a peculiar look and simply nodded in our direction. Then it was the cabby's turn to refuse to believe his eyes. TWO YOUNG THINGS LIKE US WANTING A CAB? Whatever were things coming to? Finally he condescended to ask where we wanted to go. "Plane Street," I said. It was only a few minutes' ride away so I think he decided to risk it. Into the cab we got and with a click of his tongue he set his horse trotting. No sooner had we seated ourselves in luxury than we were getting out in front of Aunt Alice's house. For that ride I paid the princely sum of two shillings, and as the cab drove off we knocked on Aunt Alice's front door.

It was opened by her daughter-in-law, who stared at us in stupefaction; no welcoming smile from her and no invitation to come inside either! "They're all down at t'Chapel," she told us in tones of high disapproval, "they're expecting you there." "Oh...well could you lend us an umbrella?" I managed to ask, much deflated. It must have seemed to her the lesser of two evils for otherwise she might have felt bound to ask us in out of the rain. She retreated inside to re-emerge with an umbrella, which she handed to us with the air of one who didn't like anything about us. (It was a feeling which we quietly reciprocated!).

41

So there we were, once more out in the rain and faced with a walk to Zion Chapel, though this time we did at least have an umbrella. Then I realised something. We could have got off that tram one stop past the station! That would have brought us right to the door of the Zion Schoolroom! What a daft thing I had done! Eventually we arrived at the schoolroom, where a crowd of people were having lunch. Arthur and the rest of our relations recognized us and after taking the umbrella to drip in an umbrella stand, he conducted us to a table where we were provided with some sorely needed sustenance. Arthur and his friends then showed us round the new buildings while the older people seemed busy meeting past acquaintances, renewing friendships etc. When Doris, silly girl, blurted out the story of the cab fiasco, Arthur and his pals howled with laughter, and who could blame them? Personally I would have preferred it to be kept a secret between Doris and myself.

Soon afterwards it was time to go into the Chapel for the Opening and Dedication Services. I cannot pretend that Doris and I were either exalted or exhilarated. Truth to tell, in fact, we were rather bored. Our new clothes, we felt, were not receiving their due attention. It was therefore a great relief to us when the proceedings came to an end and, after a further inspection of the new building, we were shepherded back to the Schoolroom where tea was being served. "Would you like to go to the pictures this evening instead of attending tonight's meeting?" suggested Arthur when tea was over. We neither of us needed any persuasion — we were both ready and most willing!

The picture house was almost next door and we were on the point of entering it when I suddenly remembered the umbrella. Arthur said he would go back for it. "What sort of handle had it?" he asked. In those days there were no coloured umbrellas; they were all black, and the only feature by which they could be distinguished was the handle. Goodness, I'd never noticed the handle, but remembering Sannie, I felt sure that any umbella owned by her would have a silver handle. Accordingly I said I thought that it was silver. Back went Arthur therefore to return with the precious umbrella. As we came out of the the picture house we were relieved to find that the rain had stopped and, after leaving Doris at a friend's house where she was to sleep that night, we reached Aunt Alice's about eleven o'clock.

As Arthur and I went in we found ourselves confronted by the entire household. There they all were, his brother, John Willie, Sannie, Aunt Alice, Auntie Lizzie and Gladys, all looking as if the end of the world were in sight and they held us responsible. "Where have you been and what do you mean by coming in at this time?" shouted J.W., furious that we had gone to the pictures instead of staying for the evening meeting. To think that at that time Arthur was twenty-two — anyone might have thought we had been out all night! After ranting on for some time, J.W. ended by shouting: "And where's Sannie's umbrella?" "Here it is," I replied, holding the umbrella up triumphantly — thank goodness I had remembered it! He took one look at it and nearly went apopleptic. "That's not Sannie's," he yelled, "Sannie's has an ivory handle." He was in one of the vile tempers for which he was well known, and he raved on about how the umbrella was a twenty-first birthday present from his late father to Sannie. The tirade continued for some time, during which all I could do was to interpolate "sorry" at intervals. At length Aunt Alice quietly suggested that we should all go to bed, which suited everyone but J.W. I think he was enjoying himself in a sadistic sort of way.

The next morning Aunt Alice greeted us with the glad news that Sannie's umbrella had been returned. A neighbour living in the same street had, it seemed, recognised it when it had been left behind at the schoolroom instead of hers. That sort of neighbour was typical of the Bacup of those days! All was well, therefore, but there was a lingering sense of unpleasantness in the house. However, it was another day and fine too, so Arthur and I went to collect Doris and we set off to walk to the Chapel. On our way there Doris and I were pleased to notice that people were turning round to look at us. At last, we felt, justice was being done! Up to that point there had been little opportunity to display our finery, but now Bacup seemed ready for us. Seldom, we were sure, had the natives seen such a display of up-to-date elegance. "Nay, Pickup, where has ta picked them up? I'd raffle them off!" shouted a group of small boys after us, but such was our folly that far from being annoyed, we were actually gratified by this. Arthur was quite amused. Perhaps he thought that some of our radiance reflected on him!

That evening when we returned to Oswaldtwistle, I think we were both feeling that apart from the incident of the umbrella, it had been a fitting outing for the coming season's fashions. Father never asked for particulars of how the sovereign had been divided, but even if I had told him I think he would only have been amused.

Chapter 12

Working in Blackburn

Before I was married I obtained a post as head dressmaker in a small establishment in Blackburn. It was a corner shop in a working-class district near Mill Hill. The proprietress was a Mrs Annie Hocking. Her husband was a lorry driver on the railway and they had two small boys. She was a thoroughly kind and amiable woman, but to say that she was easy-going was to endow her with a higher degree of energy than she really possessed. She had been brought up on a small farm in the country and her vocabulary included some strange terms, three of which spring to mind. She spoke of "agestive" (adhesive) plasters, "permagannet of potash", and the district named Fylde she pronounced "Flyde". Ruth, the apprentice, was a nice girl of about fifteen with dark curly hair who lived out in the country beyond Blackburn. Although her education at a village school had been rather poor, she was quite intelligent in her dressmaking work. We got on well together, though I do remember one occasion when she was not best pleased with me. There were only the two of us in the workroom so we used to chatter away to one another on any subject that came into our heads. One day, thinking that it would amuse her, I told her the following (quite true) tale, which took place years before the First World War.

A cousin of Tom's named Abel, together with his wife Martha, had arranged to go for a short holiday with a couple of friends, Bob Walsh and his wife. On arriving at their destination they found, to their consternation, that they had to share a bedroom. In those days that was not so unusual, but nevertheless they felt somewhat annoyed. However, they had no option but to accept the situation. After some little discussion it was arranged that the women should go to bed first and the men would follow later, getting undressed in the dark.

This plan they put into operation and at first all went smoothly. Martha, however, being a particularly shy young woman, resolved to get up in the morning before anyone else was awake so that no one would see her getting dressed. At the time of which I am speaking, bathrooms were almost unheard of and most visitors never expected them. There was a simple toilet jug filled with cold water together with a basin on the wash-hand stand. About half an hour before breakfast time the maid would usually bring another jug, this time of hot water, and leave it outside the bedroom door. On this occasion Martha did not wait for the jug of hot water; instead she hurriedly performed her ablutions in cold. After breakfast, while taking a stroll on the promenade, Abel noticed that Martha seemed decidedly worried and ill at ease. When he asked her what the matter was she replied: "I don't like sleeping in that room. I got up early to get a bit of privacy while I was getting washed and dressed and — would you believe it? — every time I looked, Bob was peeping at me. He was pretending to be asleep but he had one eye open all the time." At this Abel roared with laughter. "Why, you daftie," he exclaimed, "didn't you know that Bob has one glass eye?" I waited for Ruth to laugh, but after remaining quiet for a second or two she said: "D'you know, I never realised before that people could see with glass eyes." I was so surprised at this reaction that I said without thinking: "Well, what's the good of getting a glass eye if you can't see with it?" Nothing more was said on the subject, but that evening when she went home for tea she re-told the story to her family. The reaction of both her father and her elder brother was to roar with laughter and scoff at her for being so 'dumb'. As a result, next day when she came to work she was thoroughly annoyed with me and would scarcely speak unless she had to.

Soon after this we took on another apprentice, a girl named Martha. Though not very bright, she was always eager to please. At that time most of the girls working in the mills wore black aprons made of a special type of shiny cotton material called Black Italian cloth. It was almost like cheap satin and was very hard-wearing. Provided we were not too busy in the workroom, we used to make such aprons to order for the shop. One day Mrs Hocking wanted half a dozen made but found we were out of the material. "Do you know where my mother's shop is at Ewood?" she asked Martha, and Martha assured her that she did. "Well, continued Mrs H., "I want you to go and ask my mother to send me some Black Italian — I'll let her have some of mine when the next order comes in." Off went Martha, pleased, no doubt, to be getting out of the workroom for a time, but she returned without any material. "Not got any?" exclaimed Mrs H. in perplexity, "Why, she had a whole roll when I was down there last week!" "Well, she hasn't got any now," retorted Martha, "she looked all through her cupboards in the kitchen and the living-room." "Cupboards in the kitchen?" rejoined a puzzled Mrs H., "She would never have any there — what in the world did you ask for?" "What you told me to ask for," answered Martha, "Black Spanish." In case any of my readers have never heard of Black Spanish, I should explain that it was kept in most households during the winter as a cure for coughs and colds!

From time to time a man who was deaf and dumb used to come round, ostensibly selling tracts of a religious kind but in reality begging. He also wore blue glasses and pretended to be blind. Very well known in the district, he was rumoured to be quite well off, living in a large house in one of the well-to-do areas. He also had a name as a 'womaniser' and many of the women in the neighbourhood were somewhat afraid of him. If all that was said of him was true, I cannot imagine how he could have got away with it all. At all events this was what we believed about him.

One afternoon Mrs H., having occasion to go out, asked us to attend to the shop while she was away. Our workroom was over the shop and through a small hole in the floor we could see anyone who came in. When the shop bell rang, Ruth looked through the hole. "It's the dummie," she exclaimed in a startled voice. ('The dummie' was the name by which the man was known in the district). "I'm not going down," she went on, so it was left to me to cope. Mrs H.'s usual practice was to put tuppence in his hand and off he would go. I used to say how silly she was to encourage him and that I wouldn't give him a cent. Now was the chance to prove my words. Ruth wouldn't go down so I must. I bravely started down the stairs but then a thought struck me: how does one say 'no thankyou' to a deaf and dumb man who is also supposed to be blind?

By this time I was in the shop and, deaf, blind or not, he knew I was there. He stepped towards me, one hand filled with his tracts, the other stretched out towards me. I took hold of his free arm, pulled him towards the door, opened it, and gently pushed him outside. Then I closed the door and returned to the workroom. I expect he was surprised at the strange way in which he had been treated, for he never came again. Mrs Hocking was sincerely thankful; she had never known how to say 'no'. After all, how could she if he was deaf? I doubt if he would get away with such a ploy today, and even in those days I am surprised that he managed it.

Chapter 13

It Looked So Easy

After I got off the tram from Oswaldtwistle I had quite a long walk to get to my work in Blackburn. The first part of the walk was the most interesting; it was along Darwen Street which had shops on either side. On Saturday I finished my work at one o'clock and one Saturday, as I was on my way home, I noticed that there was a sale on at a music shop which I had to pass. I stopped to look in the window and saw a violin marked three pounds. Now for many years I had fancied the idea of being a violinist. I already played the piano a bit, and imagined that it would be quite easy for me to pick up the knack of playing the violin. Oh what ignorance!

I thought I could just about manage the three pounds which would enable me to achieve my ambition, so I boldly entered the shop. A man came forward to serve me and I asked to look at the violin in the window which was marked £3. He fetched it out and I, knowing less than nothing about such instruments, thought it looked the right shape and noted that it had its full complement of strings. However, thinking that I ought not to appear too eager, I asked if the case was included in the price. By this time the man had summed me up as a complete ignoramus — a 'sucker' in fact — so he assured me that not only was the case included but that he would 'throw in' the bow as well. Ignoring the violin, he spent some time telling me what a good bow I would be getting, "quite up to standard, that is," he assured me. I agreed to buy the violin, bow and case for three pounds and left the shop proudly carrying my 'bargain' under my arm. How happy I felt! I realise now how happy the man must have felt too! If you play the piano or sing, no one can tell just by seeing you in the street that you are a musician, but to be seen carrying a violin case — obviously that marks you out at once as a violinist...Well, doesn't it?

When I reached home I went quietly in at the front door and straight upstairs to my bedroom, which was at the top of the house. I shut the door and then, for the first time, handled my precious instrument. Tentatively I drew the bow across the strings several times. Straightway the thought struck me that this was not going to be as easy as I had contemplated. Obviously it was going to be some time before I was ready to play on any concert platform, however good my bow. The noise it produced was certainly weird.

Later I was told how the family had reacted downstairs. "Good heavens, what was that?" asked my mother, hearing the 'funny noise', "it sounds like the cat somewhere upstairs. Go and see whether it has got shut into one of the bedrooms." Following the noise, my sister Dorothy began to ascend the attic stairs just at the moment when I opened the door. I had decided that the time had come to display my bargain to the family. What utter amazement it caused! They were absolutely dumbfounded. Doubts as to my sanity began to show on their faces.

In time they got used to it and as the months went by I managed to reach a point at which I was able to scrape a hymn tune or two — 'scrape' being the operative word. I would bribe Dorothy to accompany my efforts on the piano, which helped to drown the many squeaks and false notes. Even she, however, kind girl though she was, could only stand so much. In the end she found it more than she could bear; she refused to play for me any more.

At intervals I would still try to 'have a go' by myself, but such occasions became more and more spasmodic, less and less frequent until at last I all but forgot the wretched thing.

After I was married and my son was about two years old, I decided to try again. The second time I took the violin out of its case and started to tune it my small son looked up at me with tears rolling down his face. "No, Mummy," he said pitifully, "No!" That did it! That was my Waterloo! That too was the last time I was ever to pose a threat to Yehudi Menuhin. Strange to say, a friend offered to buy the violin and I sold it to her for two pounds. For the price of one pound I had learnt one of life's bitterest lessons: I had limitations; there were things I couldn't do. Oh well — I was young then!

48